Gospel Truth for kids
(and grown-ups)

Discover the very best **FREE GIFT** you can ever receive

TB Bailie

First published 2024 by Broncle Publications
www.broncle.com
Copyright © 2024 Thomas Brian Bailie
All rights reserved

Cover photograph, iStock.com/Serp77
Quoted text from ESVUK, The Holy Bible English Standard Version Copyright © 2001 by Crossway Bibles, a division of Good News Publishers.
Used by permission.
All rights reserved.

ISBN: 9798874056575
Imprint: Independently published

Other books by the same author

Bible Milk & Honey
But if Not
Bible Nuts & Bolts
Kircubbin (and hereabouts)
成功企业的销售和营销秘笈
Raising a Smile
The Broncle
Prepare Yourself for China
Alzheimer's Timeline

For our grandchildren,
with thanks to Cedric,
and to Jim, sower and waterer of seeds.

God's word is precious and inspiring, and overwhelming and wonderful to me.

By his grace, God has blessed me with the ability to communicate in writing; and, I shall use this gift that God may be glorified.

By God's good grace, may this book be a blessing to your understanding of the truth, and to all those with whom you share it.

I pray a blessing over you dear reader:

That the God of our Lord Jesus Christ, the Father of glory, may give you a spirit of wisdom and of revelation in the knowledge of him, having the eyes of your heart enlightened, that you may know what is the hope to which he has called you.

And, may God be glorified in your life and testimony.

Be blessed.

Amen

Foreword for parents

Among the friendly bustle of Portaferry market one sunny spring morning, I noticed a friend frowning fearfully.
I asked what was upsetting him.
He pointed towards his grandchildren who were happily playing nearby; sighing, he shook his head and exclaimed, *"Brian, what kind of a troubled world are these beautiful young children growing up into?"*

My reply assured him that his grandchildren were born for such a time as this, by God's good will; and, that it is up to us, as parents and grandparents, to make sure that our little ones are taught the truth of God's Word, that they might know Jesus Christ as their Lord and their Saviour; because, God has already prepared a plan for each of our children to fulfil in their lifetime, to God's good purpose.

But Jesus called unto him saying, "Let the children come to me, and do not hinder them, for to such belongs the kingdom of God." Luke chapter 18, verse 16

In Matthew chapter 13, Jesus taught a parable about a sower who went out to sow seeds.

Some of the seeds fell on the hard path where the birds easily ate them up.

Some of the seeds fell on ground that was shallow and rocky; but when the weather got hot and dry, the maturing plants quickly withered and died.

Some of the seeds fell among thorny weeds; but, when those seeds began to grow, the thorny weeds grew up quicker, and smothered them.

Other seeds fell on good soil: some of these seeds produced a harvest of 100 grains, some 60 grains, and some 30 grains.

The seed is the Word of God, and the sower is the person who shares the Word of God. The different places where the seeds fell are the different conditions of the people's hearts that hear the Word of God.

This truth makes children very special, because their hearts have not yet become impenetrable like the hard path, nor superficial like the shallow rocky soil, nor smothered in the cares of the world like the thorny patch.

Less corrupted by the world, the hearts of children are more open to receive the truth of God's Word.

The world is trying harder and harder to corrupt our children: to pollute them with lies, and convince them that good is bad, and bad is good.

For this reason it is important that children are taught the gospel truth sooner, than later.
This is my motivation for writing this book. And may it be the reason why you read it to your children, and encourage them to read it too.

Today is another day closer to the season of suffering preceding the return of Jesus Christ: it is essential that the gospel message is shared with our children so that they may know the truth: so that they may take up the whole armour of God, and be able to withstand the evil day; and, having done all, to stand firm in the truth of Jesus Christ.

I sought the Lord, and he answered me and delivered me from all my fears. Those who look to him are radiant, and their faces shall never be ashamed.
Psalm 34, verses 4 and 5

GOSPEL TRUTH FOR KIDS

Chapters

For such a time as this	1
The gospel truth	5
Is the Bible true?	11
Who is God?	21
What is sin?	27
Who is Jesus?	31
No more death!	39
Muddles and troubles	45
Your Free Gift	53
Holy Spirit	61
A new life	63
Following Jesus	75
God's will for your life	79
Any questions	87
1 John	91

GOSPEL TRUTH FOR KIDS

For such a time as this

The world is muddled and troubled. It can be very difficult to know *what* the truth is, or *who* you can trust.

You are growing up in a world where important leaders often don't know what the truth is!

But, you were not born by accident. God knew all about you, even before you were born.

Your eyes saw my unformed substance; in your book were written, every one of them, the days that were formed for me, when as yet there was none of them. Psalm 139, verse 16

Before you were born, God had already written his good plan for your life in his book.

And, because God has already written a plan for your life, you are able to grow up strong and sure once you put your trust in God.

You have a choice:
- *Either,* you can try to live your life *without God*, and forget about his good plan for your life.
- *Or,* you can live your life *with God*, for the good purpose that God has already planned for you.

Living *without God* means that you will need to place your hope in other people, and trust that they are telling the truth and leading you in the right way.

Living *with God* means that you will know the truth; it means that you can enjoy a hope that is certain; it means that you can walk boldly and confidently in the world, because God is truth.

Lead me in your truth and teach me, for you are the God of my salvation; for you I wait all the day long. **Psalm 25 verse 5**

When you know that the forecast is for wet and wintery weather, you prepare by taking shelter, or by protecting yourself with warmer clothes.

Likewise, when you know that there are muddles and troubles ahead, you need to prepare yourself by sheltering in God's truth, and protecting yourself with God's good promises.

Behold, God is my salvation; I will trust, and not be afraid; for the Lord God is my strength and my song, and he has become my salvation.
Isaiah chapter 12, verse 2

Realise the truth that you were *not* born by chance.

For God's good purpose, *you* were born for such a time as this.

Muddles and troubles will happen, (they happen to everyone); but, the bigger you make God in your life, the smaller your problems will be.

Never feel that you are unimportant: God often uses little people to do big things for Him.

But God chose what is foolish in the world to shame the wise; God chose what is weak in the world to shame the strong.
1 Corinthians chapter 1, verse 27

In your Bible, you will read about a boy called *David*.
But, even though David was just a shepherd *boy*, God recognised David *as a man*.

I have found in David the son of Jesse a man after my own heart, who will do all my will.
Acts chapter 13, verse 22

David's family saw: a shepherd boy.
God saw: a king, a warrior, a poet, a leader: God saw a **giant-killer**.

What does God see in you?

The gospel truth

The Bible has a special word for *good news*. It's called the *gospel.*

This good news is the most important message you will ever be told.

The gospel message explains that God has already sent a very special person to save you from your sins and the worries of this muddled and troubled world.

This is good, and it is pleasing in the sight of God our Saviour, who desires all people to be saved and to come to the knowledge of the truth. 1 Timothy chapter 2, verses 3 and 4

In the beginning, God created the world. And God created the first man, and gave him life.

God gave the man a rule to keep. And, God told the man that the punishment for breaking the rule was that he would eventually die.

But the man was tricked by a lie; and because the man believed the lie, the man broke God's rule.
Breaking one of God's rules is called a sin.

Because the man broke God's rule, the man would eventually die.
But, because the man was the very first man, everyone in the whole world is related to him; and because we are all related to the first man, we have all inherited his nature.

The first man's nature was to sin.
Because we are all related to the first man, it is our nature to sin too.
It is sin that has made the world so muddled and troubled.

But, God loved the world so much, that he sent his only Son, so that everyone who believes in him should not die because of their sin, but can live forever.

So, God sent his Son into the world.
But, God's Son had to come into the world in a very special way.
God's Son had to be born without a man as his natural father.
So, God used a miracle to form his Son within a young woman who gave birth to him.

It was very important that God's Son was created this way, because it meant that God's Son did not inherit the first man's nature to sin.

God's Son was born clean from sin, and he lived without ever *thinking* a sin, or *saying* a sin, or *doing* a sin.
God's Son lived a perfect life.
This was very important, because God needed a perfect person to accept the punishment for all of the sins of everyone who would ever believe in him.

God's Son accepted the *blame* for all of your sins.
And, God's Son accepted the *punishment* for all of your sins when he was killed on a cross.

This means that you can be saved from the punishment that you deserve for your sins, because God's Son has already taken the blame and suffered the punishment that you deserve.

Because of this amazing act of love, God can treat you as if you have lived the perfect life without sin that his Son lived.

But there's more: Because God's Son came back to life three days after he was killed on a cross, it means that God's Son has also broken the curse of death that the first man began.

For God so loved the world, that he gave his only Son, that whoever believes in him should not perish but have eternal life.
John chapter 3, verse 16

The gift of eternal life with God is *very* good news!
It's called the Gospel.

You have a choice:

- *Either*, you can ignore God's loving gift of his Son, and all that he has done for you; and you can keep following the ways of the world.
- *Or*, you can accept God's loving gift of his Son, and be washed clean from all of your sins; and you can look forward to a wonderful eternal life with God.

God's only Son is called Jesus.

Jesus said, "I am the way, and the truth, and the life."
John chapter 14, verse 6

Jesus is in heaven right now, sitting upon his amazing throne.

Jesus is waiting for you to accept him as your Lord and your Saviour.

For you, O Lord, are good and forgiving, abounding in steadfast love to all who call upon you. Give ear, O LORD, to my prayer; listen to my plea for grace.
Psalm 86, verses 5 and 6

You can choose to *follow the world*.
Or, you can choose to *follow Jesus*.

But, before you decide which to follow, be sure to find out *where* you are following them to!

Enter by the narrow gate. For the gate is wide and the way is easy that leads to destruction, and those who enter by it are many. For the gate is narrow and the way is hard that leads to life, and those who find it are few.
Matthew chapter 7, verses 13 and 14

Is the Bible true?

This is a very important question to know the answer to, because if the Bible is false, *what is truth?*

There are lots of religions in the world, and they all believe in a god, or some sort of creation story.
But, there can only be one true God, because there can only be one truth.

All of the other religions of the world have been invented by men. They are just superstitions and stories and legends and lies that men have made up to try to explain how and why the world was created.

When God created the first man and woman, God created them to be special, and superior to all of the other living creatures.

One of the special qualities that God created in people is our nature to worship. But, if people do not know God, how can they worship him?

If people do not know God, they start to worship other things: they make up stories and superstitions, legends and lies; they create false gods and false religions.

You can tell that those religions and gods are false, because they simply don't make sense! And the reason why they don't make sense is because they are religions and gods that were invented by men.

Nowadays, less people worship strange gods, but more people worship other things like money and fame, possessions and pleasure; and some proud people even worship themselves.

No one understands; no one seeks for God. All have turned aside; together they have become worthless; no one does good, not even one.

Romans chapter 3, verses 11 and 12

Some people do not believe in any god or any religion. These people are called *atheists*.

Atheists believe that all the stars and planets, the earth, and every thing on the earth and in the earth, animals, fish, birds, insects, plants, bacteria, fungus,... *everything*, just happened by chance!

Most atheists believe that you are related to an ape, and the ape was related to a fish, and the fish was related to some slimy stuff at the bottom of a pond. They call this slippery science, *evolution*.

But when you think about how amazing your body is, and all the creatures, and all the plants and trees, and all the planets and stars: there is order: there is purpose: there is creation: *there is a Creator*.

You know that God exists, because you can see what God has created.

For what can be known about God is plain to them, because God has shown it to them.
Romans chapter 1, verse 19

Is the Bible all true?

It might have taken as long as 1,800 years to write the Bible; and in that time it was written by about forty different people.

But in truth, just one person wrote the Bible: **God**.

God especially chose certain people to write the Bible. God inspired each of them to accurately tell the truth.

The Bible is one true and reliable message from God to you.

All scripture is breathed out by God and profitable for teaching, for reproof, for correction, and for training in righteousness.
2 Timothy chapter 3, verse 16

The first part of the Bible is called the *Old Testament*; and, the other part of the Bible is called the *New Testament*.

The Old Testament is all about the first agreement that God made with *his* people; and, the New Testament is all about the final agreement that God has made with *all* people.

Although Jesus is not mentioned by name in the first part of the Bible, the whole Bible is all about Jesus.

This is because Jesus is God's loving gift to the world: Jesus is the answer to our problem with sin.

Within the *Old Testament*, there are as many as 350 sayings about who Jesus is and what Jesus will do when he will comes.

In the *New Testament*, Jesus accurately fulfilled around half of those sayings.

Therefore, the Old Testament is true!

And, it means that you can be certain that the other half of the sayings about Jesus will also be accurately fulfilled whenever Jesus comes back to earth, because the Bible clearly tells us that Jesus Christ is coming back.

So Christ, having been offered once to bear the sins of many, will appear a second time, not to deal with sin but to save those who are eagerly waiting for him.
Hebrews chapter 9, verse 28

The wisdom of the Bible is so much greater than human wisdom. The Bible could not have been written by the efforts and skill and knowledge of people alone, not even by very, very clever people.

God directly inspired people whom God had especially chosen to write the Bible: they wrote God's words.

The wisdom and humility and grace and compassion of Jesus that is described in the Bible, is beyond all human reasoning.

The only possible explanation is that Jesus really is who he says he is: Jesus truly is the Son of God.

Long ago, at many times and in many ways, God spoke to our fathers by the prophets, but in these last days he has spoken to us by his Son, whom he appointed the heir of all things, through whom also he created the world.

He is the radiance of the glory of God and the exact imprint of his nature.

Hebrews chapter 1, verses 1 to 3

The Bible is also packed full of other important true information.

When people used to believe that the earth was flat, the Bible said that the earth was shaped like a ball.

When people used to believe that the earth sat motionless in space and the sun and stars revolved around the earth, the Bible said that the earth spins.

We now know that the Bible was true about these things long before scientists rediscovered the truth.

There are people who explore history, who dig up ancient sites to discover treasures and clues, and lost cities and temples and palaces.

These people who explore history are called *archaeologists.*

Archaeologists still use the Bible to help them to find and explain the many amazing things that they are discovering.

Archaeologists know that the Bible is true.

Buy truth, and do not sell it.
Proverbs chapter 23, verse 23

Jesus chose some close friends to follow him when he was on earth.
These friends learnt from Jesus, and they saw many of the miracles that Jesus worked.
Some of these friends saw Jesus killed on a cross by Roman soldiers. They knew that Jesus was dead.
And then Jesus came back to life, just as the Bible had said he would.
When Jesus came back to life after being dead for three days, he was seen by over 500 people.
Jesus spoke with the people, and showed them the wounds that he had suffered when he was killed.
Jesus was fully restored to life.

"Put your finger here, and see my hands; and put out your hand, and place it in my side. Do not disbelieve, but believe."
Jesus said to him, "Have you believed because you have seen me? Blessed are those who have not seen and yet believed."
John chapter 20, verses 27 and 29

Jesus was not a ghost!

Jesus walked with people; and Jesus cooked a meal that he ate with his friends.

Jesus truly came back to life three days after he had been killed.

These friends of Jesus knew that Jesus truly is the Son of God, and they spent the rest of their lives telling the world all about the good news of Jesus, and how Jesus has provided the answer to our problem with sin.

These followers of Jesus would never have spent the rest of their lives telling the world about Jesus if Jesus wasn't the truth.

Most of these friends were killed for telling the world about Jesus: they would not have died telling the world about Jesus if Jesus wasn't the truth.

Jesus said to him, "I am the way, and the truth, and the life. No one comes unto the Father except through me."
John chapter 14, verse 6

Can I prove the Bible is true?

That's easy!

You can tell that the Bible is true, because it does what it says it does.

It changes lives.

It changed my life.

And, it can change *your* life too.

The sum of your word is truth, and every one of your righteous rules endures for ever.

Princes persecute me without cause, but my heart stands in awe of your words.

Psalm 119, verses 160 and 161

Who is God?

Everything about God is beyond human comprehension: we could never understand the wonderful immeasurable nature of God.

Many people don't want to believe in God because they are afraid of the truth: the truth is inconvenient!

Which God?
Some people believe in other gods and religions.

But the Bible explains that all other gods are false: all other gods have been created by men. People invented other gods because they did not know the one true God; they invented other gods because they needed to explain how the world was created, and where they came from.

**Their idols are silver and gold, the work of human hands.
They have mouths, but do not speak; eyes, but do not see.
They have ears, but do not hear; noses, but do not smell.
They have hands, but do not feel; feet, but do not walk; and they do not make a sound in their throat.
Those who make them become like them; so do all who trust in them.**
Psalm 115, verses 4 to 8

The gods of all the religions of the world are false, and worthless, and hopeless.
Only the one true God that you meet in your Bible is true.

Where did God come from?

God has always existed.
God exists now.
And, God will always exist.

God existed before everything.
God has no beginning because God is the beginning.

There was no time before God, because God created time!
Because God created time, God existed before time: God has existed for ever and ever, and will continue to exist for ever and ever.

I am the Alpha and the Omega, the first and the last, the beginning and the end.
Revelation chapter 22, verse 13

Alpha and Omega are the first and last letters of the Greek alphabet. God is telling us that he is the A and the Z: there was nothing before God, and there will be nothing that comes after God.

Before the mountains were brought forth, or ever you had formed the earth and the world, from everlasting to everlasting you are God.
Psalm 90, verse 2

Who is God?

A lot of people get confused about who God is, because God is three persons.

God is the *Father*.
God is the *Son*, Jesus.
And, God is the *Holy Spirit*.

But, how can three persons be one?

The answer to this question is very important to understand, because people who do not believe in God will say that you are trusting in three gods, not the one true God.

God is one **being**.
And, God is three **persons** within his one being.

What's the difference between a being, and a person?

The *being* is the quality that makes God **what he is**.
The *person* is the quality that makes God **who he is**.

God, is **what** God is.
Father, *Son*, and *Holy Spirit* are **who** God is.

Think about yourself,...
What, and *who* are you?

You are a human being.
But, there are over 8,000,000,000 other human beings in the world: and they are not *you*!
You are you.
Of all the people in the world, *you* are the only you.

I am a *human being*.
And, my name is *Brian*.
What I am, is a human being.
Who I am, is Brian.

Just like you: I am one being, (a human being); and, I am one person, (Brian).
God is one being: God; with three persons: the Father, the Son, and the Holy Spirit.

Go therefore and make disciples of all nations, baptizing them in the name of the Father and of the Son and of the Holy Spirit.
Matthew chapter 28, verse 19

Why is God three persons?

Each of the three persons of God have different roles to fulfil.

God the Father is superior to the Son and the Holy Spirit.
God the Son (Jesus) was sent into the world to do the work that God the Father had prepared for him.
God the Holy Spirit was sent into the world after Jesus, to stay here to comfort and to influence and to encourage everyone who receives Jesus as their Lord and their Saviour.

Do you not know that you are God's temple and that God's Spirit dwells in you?
1 Corinthians chapter 3, verse 16

What is sin?

Sin is breaking God's rules.
You sin every time that you *do* something that God hates, and every time that you *say* something that God hates, and even just *think* something that God hates.

The very first sin was done by the very first man. And because every one of us is related to the very first man, we have all inherited his nature to sin.

We sin because it is our nature to sin: it doesn't matter how hard you try to be perfect, it is impossible not to sin: you just can't help it!

For all have sinned and fall short of the glory of God.
Romans chapter 3, verse 23

God hates sin.
God hates sin because he is perfect and sinless and holy.

God will never tolerate sin anywhere near him, which means that you can never be with God, unless you get rid of all of your sins completely.

Some people try really, really hard to live a life without sin. These people are very, very strict in everything they do: they perform lots of very religious practices; they separate themselves from people who are not like they are; and they live a life that is completely devoted to following God's rules.

But even these people are not good enough for God.

In fact, God hates people who think that they are better than others: these people can be often be worse than a bad person who comes to God with deep regret for their sins.

The sacrifices of God are a broken spirit; a broken and contrite heart, O God, you will not despise.
Psalm 51, verse 17

It is very important to understand that there is **nothing** that you can do by your own efforts to make yourself good or acceptable to God.

Everyone is guilty of sin, and there is nothing that you can do by your own efforts to remove your sin.

Though your sins are like scarlet, they shall be as white as snow; though they are red like crimson, they shall become like wool.
Isaiah chapter 1, verse 18

Before God sent his Son into the world as Jesus Christ, the only way to deal with sin was by sacrificing animals to God.
But the blood of animals would never be good enough.
What the world needed was a perfect sacrifice that would be made once and for all time.

For this reason, and because God loved the world so much, God sent his Son, Jesus Christ, into the world to fix our problem with sin.

Christ loved us and gave himself up for us, a fragrant offering and sacrifice to God.
Ephesians chapter 5, verse 2

Jesus Christ came into the world to be the perfect sacrifice that God needed to allow him to completely forgive all of your sins.

You need to stop trying to earn your own way into God's favour. You need to realise that there is nothing you can do by your own efforts to make your sins go away.

Jesus is the **only** person who can make you right with God.
There is **no other way**: only Jesus.

There are no other religions in the world that can help you: only the truth of the Bible: Jesus is the only answer that can deal with your sin, and make you right with God.

Jesus said to him, "I am the way, and the truth, and the life. No one comes to the Father except through me."
John chapter 14, verse 6

Who is Jesus?

The whole Bible is about Jesus.
Jesus is the Son of God.
The Son of God is one of the three persons who make up the one being that is God.

Because God has always existed, and exists now, and will always exist, Jesus has always existed. This means that Jesus was there at the beginning, and at the creation of the world.

He was in the beginning with God. All things were made through him, and without him was not any thing made that was made.
John chapter 1, verses 2 and 3

Jesus is often called Jesus Christ. *Christ* is not his name: it is his title.

Christ means, chosen by God.

Jesus is very, very special: God sent Jesus into the world to fix our problem with sin.

As soon as the first man was tricked into believing a lie, which caused him to sin, God already had a plan to fix everything.

Before God sent his Son into the world to fix the problem that sin had created, the only way that people could receive a brief pardon for their sins was by making a sacrifice.

To receive a pardon for their sins, the people sacrificed their best male sheep, goats, and bulls.

These perfectly *innocent* animals were killed as a sin offering to God to pay for the *guilt* of sinful people.

But, these animal offerings to God were never enough to forgive the sins of all of the people forever.

For it is impossible for the blood of bulls and goats to take away sins.

Hebrews chapter 10, verse 4

God required a perfect sacrifice that would allow him to forgive the sins of all people, once and for all time.
God's answer to sin was to send his Son into the world, to live and to die as the one and only perfect sacrifice.

The Son of God left his throne in heaven, and came to earth, because this was God's good plan.
God's Son had to become a man, but he had to be born without a sinful man as his natural father.
So, God used a miracle to form his Son within a young woman who gave birth to him.

And the angel said to her, "Do not be afraid, Mary, for you have found favour with God. And behold, you will conceive in your womb and bear a son, and you shall call his name Jesus.
The Holy Spirit will come over you, and the power of the Most High will overshadow you; therefore the child to be born will be called holy – the Son of God."
Luke chapter 1, verses 30, 31, and 35

But the Son of God didn't arrive like a king or a superhero.

God's Son was not born into a splendid palace, or surrounded by important people.

God's Son, Jesus, was born in a shed, surrounded by animals and some very surprised shepherds.

Jesus, the Son of God, willingly left his glorious throne in heaven to come into this world as a human being.

God sent his Son to fix our problem with sin.

For I have come down from heaven, not to do my own will but the will of him who sent me.
John chapter 6, verse 38

At the right time, when Jesus was a man, he proved to everyone that he truly is the Son of God.

Jesus explained many of the great mysteries of the Bible; and Jesus performed many, many miracles, and Jesus healed everyone who asked him.

You can read all about the amazing truths that Jesus said, and all of the wonderful things that Jesus did in the first four books of the New Testament of your Bible.

These books are named for the men that God inspired to write them, and they are called: Matthew, Mark, Luke, and John.

(If you don't have a Bible, buy one; or, most churches will give you a Bible for free: just ask.)

How did Jesus sort out sin?

It was always God's good plan that the death of Jesus would be the perfect sacrifice that was needed to deal with our sin.

To him who loves us and has freed us from our sins by his blood. Revelation chapter 1, verse 5

God was pleased to allow Jesus to be the sacrifice for your sin. God was pleased because God loves you.

The only way that you can deal with your sin and become acceptable to God, is through your belief and trust, and obedience to Jesus.

The death of Jesus paid all of the punishment that you deserve for all of your sins.

This means that you can be free from sin when you admit to God that you are a sinner, and ask for the forgiveness of your sins because of the sacrifice that Jesus made for you when he was killed on a cross.

Jesus has taken the *blame* for all of your sins; and, Jesus has suffered the *punishment* that you deserve for all of your sins.

For our sake he made him to be sin who knew no sin, so that in him we might become the righteousness of God.
2 Corinthians chapter 5, verse 21

Jesus is perfectly without sin; but Jesus suffered and died as if he was *you*, a sinner.

Jesus loves you so much that he died so that you can be as perfectly clean from sin as he is.

This means that when God looks at you, he will see in you the sinless perfection of Jesus.

But, there's more,...

When the first man was tricked by a lie, and sinned by breaking God's rule, that first man was punished for his sin. Because of that sin, the man would eventually die.

Just as sin came into the world through one man, and death through sin, and so death spread to all men because all sinned.
Romans chapter 5, verse 12

And, because everyone in the world is related to that first man, everyone in the world has inherited that man's nature to sin, and everyone will eventually die.

Jesus, has provided the answer to your problem with *sin*.

And, because Jesus came back to life after he was killed on a cross, Jesus has also provided the answer to your problem with *death*.

O death, where is your victory?
O death, where is your sting?
1 Corinthians chapter 15, verse 55

If Jesus is alive, where is he?

That's a very good question.

Jesus came back to life three days after he was killed on a cross.

After Jesus came back to life from death: Jesus visited his closest followers and showed them his wounds, proving that he was made whole again; Jesus went for a long walk with two of his followers and explained important Bible truths to them; Jesus appeared to 500 other believers; and Jesus cooked a meal of fish for his closest followers, and ate with them.

40 days after coming back to life, Jesus returned to heaven.

So then the Lord Jesus, after he had spoken to them, was taken up into heaven and sat down at the right hand of God.
Mark chapter 7, verse 55

Jesus is in heaven right now, waiting to come back to take all of his followers to be with him.

No more death?

Jesus defeated death.

Coming back to life from death is called, *resurrection*.

Jesus said to her, "I am the resurrection and the life. Whoever believes in me, though he die, yet shall he live, and everyone who lives and believes in me shall never die. Do you believe this?"
John chapter 11, verses 25 and 26

The end of death is the greatest and most important event in all of human history.

If Jesus had not come back to life from death, he would have failed in the purpose that God had planned for him.

If Jesus had not come back to life from death, it would mean that we have no hope!

Jesus came back to life from death, which means that Jesus is your one and only hope.
Jesus can save you from death.
Jesus can be your Saviour.

Just believe, ask, and receive!

He will wipe away every tear from their eyes, and death shall be no more, neither shall there be mourning, nor crying, nor pain any more, for the former things have passed away.
Revelation chapter 21, verse 4

Doesn't everyone die?

When God created man and woman, God gave them some very special qualities, which means that you are very different from all other living creatures.

Then God said, "Let us make man in our image, after our likeness."
Genesis chapter 1, verse 26

If you are created in the likeness of God, what does mean for you?

God is three persons in one being. And like God, we are made to enjoy *relationship* with one another.
You are created to enjoy a close relationship with God; and, you are created to enjoy the relationship as a man and woman married together.

God is *love*. God loved you even before you were conceived! Before you knew God, God loved you.
You are created to love: it is your nature to love: because God is love.

God created all things. And, like God, you are also *creative*. Unlike all other living creatures, you are good at designing things, making things, and improving things.

And the other very special quality that makes you like God is one that most people don't realise,...

You were created to be *eternal*.

This means that you were never supposed to die!

The only reason why people die is because of the first man's sin.

For the wages of sin is death, but the free gift of God is eternal life in Christ Jesus our Lord.
Romans chapter 6, verse 23

Jesus was killed by soldiers who were expert executioners: Jesus definitely died on a cross.
But, when Jesus came back to life three days after he was killed, Jesus had defeated death, *for ever*.

For God so loved the world, that he gave his only Son, that whoever believes in him should not perish but have eternal life.

For God did not send his Son into the world to condemn the world, but in order that the world might be saved through him.

Whoever believes in him is not condemned, but whoever does not believe is condemned already, because he has not believed in the only Son of God.
John chapter 3, verses 16, 17 and 18

But, how can you not die?

You are not just a human machine! God made you very special: to enjoy relationship, like God; to love, like God; to be creative, like God; and to be eternal, like God.

You are inside your body, a bit like the way a driver is inside a car.
But when the car breaks down, the driver doesn't die! *Of course not!*
The driver just gets out of the car.

Likewise, when your body dies, your soul leaves your body.
Your soul is the part of you that makes you, *you!* You are the soul that lives inside your body.
Your soul isn't visible: you can't poke it, or take it out to look at it.

Your soul is a spirit.

You are a spiritual person who exists within a human body.

For what does it profit a man to gain the whole world and forfeit his soul? For what can a man give in return for his soul?
Mark chapter 8, verses 36 and 37

Whenever your body eventually stops working and dies, *your soul continues to live*, but your soul lives in a different place.

I have set before you life and death, blessing and curse. Therefore choose life.
Deuteronomy chapter 30, verse 19

There are only two places where your soul might go to whenever you eventually die:

- *Either*, your sins can remain *unforgiven*, and your soul will go to a place that is completely separated from God, forever.
- *Or*, you can *receive forgiveness* for your sins through Jesus, and your soul can go to live in the loving presence of God, forever.

Muddles and troubles

Most people will ask, *"If God exists, why is there so much suffering in the world?"*

This is a very important question.

The suffering in the world comes in lots of different ways.
There is: suffering that is caused by **nature**; suffering that is caused by **sickness**; and, suffering that is caused by other **people**.

There are dangerous animals and insects and plants; earthquakes and hurricanes and floods and droughts: but, God did not create the world to be a dangerous place. The natural world became a dangerous place after sin entered the world.

Before sin, everything in the world was very good.

And God saw everything that he had made, and behold, it was very good. Genesis chapter 1, verse 31

Why is there sickness?

Maybe someone you love is suffering with sickness, or an injury. And, perhaps you have been asking God to make them better; but, they are still suffering!

Poor health is not caused by God.

The first man broke God's rule; and the punishment for that sin was that he would eventually die.
And, because everyone in the world is related to that first man, we also sin, and we will also eventually die.

Therefore, just as sin came into the world through one man, and death through sin, and so death spread to all men because all sinned. Romans chapter 5, verse 12

But, healthy people don't just die!

Most people die because they have poor health that cannot be cured.

Poor health can be caused by lots of different things:
- What you eat.
- And, how much you eat.
- What you drink.
- And, how much you drink.
- How you live your life.
- And, where you live your life.
- Fear, worry, or bad attitude.
- An inherited condition.
- Taking bad drugs.
- A bad injury.
- Or, old age.

Sin has resulted in a broken world where lots of people suffer from poor health.

A joyful heart is good medicine, but a crushed spirit dries up the bones. Proverbs chapter 17, verse 22

We know that God doesn't want us to suffer from poor health, because when he was here, Jesus healed *everyone* who asked, and restored them to full health.

When Jesus wanted more people to know that he was the Son of God, he shared his miracle healing power with his twelve chosen followers.

And he called to him his twelve disciples and gave them authority over unclean spirits, to cast them out, and to heal every disease and affliction. Matthew chapter 10, verse 1

Does God heal sickness now?

There are some people who believe that God has completely healed them from sickness or injury.
But, most people will ask God to heal them, and remain sick.

Why?

Sickness continues in the world because the world is broken by sin.
In God's good timing, there will be a new heaven and a new earth!

He will wipe away every tear from their eyes, and death shall be no more, neither shall there be mourning, nor crying, nor pain any more. Revelation 21, verse 4

When my mum got sick, I prayed for her, and lots and lots of her friends prayed for her too.
But she continued to get worse, and worse.
God didn't heal my mum. But, God lovingly cared for my mum.
God made sure that my mum was safe and nourished, comfortable and peaceful, right to the very end.
It wasn't God's plan to cure my mum. But I thank God for his love, and the continual care that God poured out upon her throughout all of her illness.

Your eyes saw my unformed substance; in your book were written, every one of them, the days that were formed for me, when as yet there was none of them. Psalm 139, verse16

God created you.
God loves you.
God has a good purpose for you.
And, before you were born, God had written down the length of your life, to his good purpose.

Why does God allow bad things to happen?

The world is muddled and troubled.

God knows how muddled the world is, and God knows all about the troubles of the world.
God knows, because God has allowed those troubles to happen!

Why?

It's very simple: the world turned its back on God; so, God turned his back on the world.

God has already shown the world how much he loves us by sending Jesus to fix our problem with sin.

And we have seen and testify that the Father has sent his Son to be the Saviour of the world.
1 John chapter 4, verse 14

God didn't ignore the world: God gave his Son to save the world!
But, even when Jesus was on earth healing, and working miracles, and teaching people the truth: only very few people believed in him.

God has already done everything that needs to be done to sort out all of the problems in the world.

All of the problems of the world were sorted once and forever whenever Jesus died on a cross and came back to life three days later.

But, why do we continue to suffer?
Because, God is waiting!

God is waiting so that more people can be saved from their sins.

The Lord is not slow to fulfil his promise as some count slowness, but is patient towards you, not wishing that any should perish, but that all should reach repentance. 1 Peter chapter 3, verse 9

Now: good news; and, bad news!

The *good news* is that today is one day closer to when everyone who knows Jesus as their Lord and Saviour will go to be with him.

The *bad news* is that the world will get worse, and worse until that day comes.

But, the best news of all is that you do not need to worry about the world getting worse; because, when you know Jesus as your Lord and your Saviour, there isn't anything that can take you away from him.

You will need to continue to live in the world, and deal with the muddles and troubles of the world. But, because you belong to Jesus, you will not belong to the world anymore.

Whenever you make Jesus the Lord of your life, you belong to him; and there isn't anything that can separate you from God's love.

For I am sure that neither death nor life, nor angels nor rulers, nor things present nor things to come, nor powers, nor height nor depth, nor anything else in all creation, will be able to separate us from the love of God in Christ Jesus our Lord.

Romans chapter 8, verses 38 and 39

Your Free Gift

Are you a good person?
I expect you might say, *Yes!*
But you would only be comparing yourself to a bad person! *Right?*

Compared to a bank robber, you are a good person.
But when you are compared to God?
God is perfect.

Even if you have only ever told one silly little lie in your whole life, compared to the perfection of God, you are bad.

For whoever keeps the whole law but fails in one point has become accountable for it all.
James chapter 2, verse 10

And, this is why you need Jesus.

Compare two types of people:
- Foolish people.
- And, true followers of Jesus.

Which type do you want to be like?

Fools, think that they are *good*.
Followers know that they are *bad*.

Fools think that heaven is for people who make themselves *worthy*.
Followers know that heaven is only for people who know that they are *unworthy*.

Fools *proudly* think that God will thank them for trying to be good.
Followers *humbly* thank God for his forgiveness.

Fools think that they can *earn* forgiveness and eternal life by their good works.
Followers know that forgiveness and eternal life is a *gift* from God that they do not deserve.

For by grace you have been saved through faith. And this is not your own doing; it is a gift of God, not a result of works, so that none can boast.

Ephesians chapter 2, verses 8 and 9

The first man broke God's rule; and the punishment for that sin was that he would eventually die.
And, because everyone in the world is related to that first man, we also sin, and we will also eventually die.

For all have sinned and fall short of the glory of God.
Romans chapter 3, verse 23

The Good News
The best good news is that God sent Jesus: Jesus is God's only Son.

Because of the good sinless *life* that Jesus lived on earth, and because of the *death* that Jesus suffered on a cross, and because of the *resurrection* of Jesus when he came back to life three days after he was killed: *You can be saved.*

You can be saved from your sin, and you can be saved from death.

For the wages of sin is death, but the free gift of God is eternal life in Christ Jesus our Lord.
Romans chapter 6, verse 23

What is Grace?

Grace is important to understand.
Grace is the opposite of *Reward*.
Grace is receiving something that you do not deserve.
Reward is receiving something that you have earned.

If you painted my fence, I might reward you with £100.
But, what if I just gave you £100, and I didn't expect you to do anything for it?
That's what you call a gift.

Just because God loves you, God can save you because of the finished work of Jesus: it is God's *gift* to you.

It is *absolutely impossible* for you to earn favour with God to save yourself from your sins.

It doesn't matter how hard you work: you can never buy grace.

But if it is by grace, it is no longer on the basis of works; otherwise grace would not be grace.
Romans chapter 11, verse 6

How can you be saved from sin and death?

Jesus died on a cross as the perfect sacrifice that God needed to allow the forgiveness of all of the sins of everyone who will ever receive Jesus as their Lord and their Saviour.

- Do you need an application form? *No!*
- Do you need to be interviewed? *No!*
- Do you need to sit an exam? *No!*
- Can you just ask?

Yes!

Because, if you confess with your mouth that Jesus is Lord and believe in your heart that God raised him from the dead, you will be saved.

For with the heart one believes and is justified, and with the mouth one confesses and is saved.

Romans chapter 10, verses 9 and 10

How can you be saved?

Jesus has already done everything for you, which means that you can be saved in three simple steps,...

1. Believe.
2. Ask.
3. Receive.

Believe

Believe that you are a *sinner*.

Believe that you must be *free from sin* to be with God.

Believe that you can never earn forgiveness for your sins *by your own efforts*.

Believe that *Jesus is the Son of God*, who came into the world to save you from all of your sins.

Believe that Jesus *accepted the blame* for all of your sins; and Jesus *suffered the punishment* that you deserve for all of your sins.

Believe that when Jesus was killed on a cross, *Jesus paid in full* the punishment for all of your sins.

Everyone who believes in him will not be put to shame.
Romans chapter 10, verse 11

Ask

This is the most important prayer you will ever make: *you must ask with your whole heart*.

Find somewhere quiet where you can be alone.
Bow your head in respect, because you are about to speak with Jesus who is the King of all kings, and the Lord of all lords.

Tell Jesus that you *believe* that he is the Son of God.
Tell Jesus that you are sorry and *ashamed* for all of the times when you have *done* something or *said* something or *thought* something that made God unhappy.
Ask Jesus to *forgive* you.
Thank Jesus for taking the punishment for all of your sins when he was killed on a cross.

If we confess our sins, he is faithful and just to forgive us our sins and to cleanse us from all unrighteousness.
1 John chapter 1, verse 9

Receive

Receive Jesus as your Saviour.

Ask, and it will be given to you; seek, and you will find; knock, and it will be opened to you. For everyone who asks receives, and the one who seeks finds, and to the one who knocks it will be opened.
Luke chapter 11, verses 9 and 10

Receive the Holy Spirit as your guide and comforter.

God's love has been poured into our hearts through the Holy Spirit who has been given to us.
Romans chapter 5, verse 5

The Holy Spirit is the third person of God.
Holy Spirit is God.
God lives in your heart!

Do you not know that you are God's temple and that God's Spirit dwells in you?
1 Corinthians chapter 3, verse 16

Holy Spirit

Or do you not know that your body is a temple of the Holy Spirit within you, whom you have from God? You are not your own, for you were bought with a price. So glorify God in your body.
1 Corinthians chapter 6, verses 19 and 20

When Jesus was killed on a cross, he paid the price for all of your sins.

Before you are saved from your sins, you belong to the sinful world.
After you are saved from your sins, you belong to Jesus.
When you are saved, Jesus will send the Holy Spirit *to live inside you.*

He who is in you is greater than he who is in the world.
1 John 4, verse 4

Repent and be baptized every one of you in the name of Jesus Christ for the forgiveness of your sins, and you will receive the gift of the Holy Spirit.
Acts chapter 2, verse 38

Holy Spirit helps you to *love* God.
Holy Spirit helps you to *obey* God.
Holy Spirit helps you to *praise* God.

For all who are led by the Spirit of God are sons of God.
Romans chapter 8, verse 14

The world will try to tempt you with things that look nice or seem fun: but often, those will be things that God hates.
Holy Spirit will help to influence you in every decision you make, and in every word you speak.
You just need to learn to listen as you study your Bible.

Teach me to do your will, for you are my God!
Let your Spirit lead me on level ground!
Psalm 142, verse 10

A new life

I was the last boy to leave school that day. I'd been kept in detention (again) for bad behaviour (again).
At 3:20pm, my teacher released me, and I chuckled to myself as I scuttled down the empty corridor.
But then I was overwhelmed.
I stood still. And, I wasn't smiling.
I was deeply ashamed of myself.
I was crushed by my guilt.

I believed in Jesus, and I knew why he was born, and why he was killed, and why he came back to life.
I *believed*, but I was not *saved*.

In my deep, deep shame, I stopped what I was doing, and quietly cried:
God, I'm ashamed. Please forgive me.

In that instant, I was saved!

I was saved in that gloomy school corridor; my hands were all grubby, my uniform was all scruffy, but it didn't matter. I was saved that afternoon in June 1974, three months before my 11th birthday.

It seems like a lifetime ago.
It seems like yesterday.

And, thinking about it now still causes me to blub a little.
Because, Jesus has changed my life.

I was already privileged.
I had been adopted when I was a baby, and I had enjoyed a very happy childhood with lots of toys and friends. My mum and dad loved me, and my brother and my sister. We lived in a big house right beside the sea; and we had nice holidays, and lots of treats and fun.

But when Jesus saved me, none of those other things mattered.
Even though I didn't understand most of the Bible, I knew that Jesus had changed my life, and I knew that the change was good.

And you, who once were alienated and hostile in mind, doing evil deeds, he has now reconciled in his body of flesh by his death, in order to present you holy and blameless and above reproach before him.
Colossians chapter 1, verses 21 and 22

You will instantly know when you are saved.
(I was supernaturally overwhelmed.)
You will realise a change in your heart and in your thoughts.
You will realise peace: you will know that you are right with God.

It will be your nature to want to worship God in everything you do.

It will be your nature to run to God for help when danger threatens.

And, it will be your nature to want to learn more and more from God's word.

For the word of God is living and active, sharper than any two-edged sword.
Hebrews chapter 4, verse 12

Read your Bible

The Bible is God's message to you.

You speak to God when you pray.
And, *God speaks to you* as you read his word, the Bible.

Before you read your Bible, ask God to help you to understand his message for you.
The Bible is God's message that was written by men that God especially inspired by his Holy Spirit.

No prophecy was ever produced by the will of man, but men spoke from God as they were carried along by the Holy Spirit.
2 Peter chapter 1, verse 21

Because the Bible was written through God's Holy Spirit, God's Holy Spirit can help you to understand your Bible.
Just ask in prayer before you read.

Trust in the LORD with all your heart, and do not lean on your own understanding.
Proverbs chapter 3, verse 5

Find a Bible translation that you can understand.

The Bible was originally written in Hebrew, Greek, and Aramaic.

Like most people, I can't read any of those languages; however, there are hundreds of English translations to choose from.

I like *The Passion Translation*, which is easy to read, and includes lots of explanations. However, I'm not sure if the whole Bible is available in this version yet.

The verses used in this book are from the *English Standard Version*, which is a close translation from the original Bible manuscripts.

A lot of churches seem to use the *New International Version*, which is written in modern-day English and is fairly easy to follow.

Another popular modern version is the *New Living Translation*.

I enjoy the *King James Version*, but the 400-year old English can be a bit difficult to follow sometimes.

How should you read your Bible?

Lots of people skip about the Bible reading a sentence here, and another sentence there.

Reading in bits like that can be confusing, and it can be difficult to understand God's message when it's not read in context:
- Who said what?
- Why was it said?
- When was it said?
- Where was it said?
- Who was it said to?

If you want to understand the Bible properly, study it like any other book: start at the beginning, and read through to the end.

All scripture is breathed out by God and profitable for teaching, for reproof, for correction, and for training in righteousness, that the man of God may be competent, equipped for every good work.
2 Timothy chapter 3, verses 16 and 17

Throughout this book there are many Bible verses that help to prove the gospel truth. It has been very important that each verse is used correctly and within context.

It is a serious problem is when the Bible is quoted incorrectly. This is called *misinterpretation*, and it can easily cause *misunderstanding*. This is why it is very important to read a whole section of the Bible at a time, and not just random verses.

And when they had read it, they rejoiced because of its encouragement.
Acts chapter 15, verse 31

If the Bible seems like too big of a job to read in one go: you're right, *but don't give up!*

To help you (by kind permission of the publishers), the New Testament letter of 1 John has been included with this book.

1 John is a short letter of just five chapters that you can read within 30-minutes; 1 John will confirm many of the gospel truths that have already been explained in this book.

Read 1 John right through from start to finish all at once.

Then, the next day read 1 John all over again, and the next day; and keep reading 1 John every day *for a whole month!*

By the end of that month you will know the valuable truths contained within 1 John better than many pastors: you will have 1 John within your mind and within your heart.

I write these things to you who believe in the name of the Son of God that you may know that you have eternal life.

1 John chapter 5, verse 13

And then, choose another book of the Bible to read in the same way.

When you read a longer book of the Bible, just split it into 30-minute reading sections.

Reading your Bible over and over again like this is not just helpful to your understanding: it is one of the best ways to allow the Holy Spirit to fill you with the joy and confidence of Jesus as your Lord and Saviour.

Talk with God

It is an honour to talk with God.
Most of your prayers may be filled with thanking God for providing for you, protecting you, guiding you, and even correcting you.

As a follower of Jesus, you can pray to God *in the name of Jesus*.
Praying *in Jesus' name* means that you understand that you have direct access to God in prayer because of the finished work of Jesus, who paid the punishment for your sins, and has made you acceptable to God.

Christ Jesus is the one who died – more than that, who was raised – who is at the right hand of God, who is indeed interceding for us.
Romans chapter 8, verse 34

When you pray *in Jesus' name*, Jesus is right beside God the Father, *pleading* on your behalf: God will hear your prayer because of all that Jesus has done, and continues to do for you through your prayers.

If you ask God for something, ask for things that Jesus would ask for: pray *according to God's will*: pray for things that reflect God's purpose, (not your own selfish purposes).

You do not have, because do not ask. You ask and do not receive, because you ask wrongly, to spend it on your passions.
James chapter 4, verses 2 and 3

Do not be discouraged when your prayers seem to be ignored: God will always have a good reason to delay, or work his purposes in other ways.

Or, perhaps *you* are preventing God from responding to your prayers because you are living in a way that makes God unhappy.

And this is the confidence we have towards him, that if we ask anything according to his will he hears us. And if we know that he hears us in whatever we ask, we know that we have the requests that we asked of him.
1 John chapter 5, verses 14 and 15

Recognise that God has already planned a good purpose for your life. Ask God to reveal his purpose for your life; and, submit to God's will. Trust that God knows what is best. And, pursue God's good purpose for your life with your whole heart and mind and spirit.

I cry out to God Most High, to God who fulfils his purpose in me.
Psalm 57, verse 2

Stumbling

Throughout all of my life I can clearly recognise God's loving hand upon me: preparing me, providing for me, protecting me, guiding me, correcting me, and shaping me.

Since Jesus saved me as a boy, I have not always walked close to God: there were times when I tried to take my own path, and make my own way, or follow the world.

Therefore, I speak from experience, assuring you that *with God* is a far better way to live, than *without God*.

Despite my countless sins and frequent failings, God is my strength and my sure hope, my guide and my comforter: my God, in Him will I trust.

If you, O LORD, should mark iniquities, O Lord, who could stand?

But with you there is forgiveness, that you may be feared.

I wait for the Lord, my soul waits, And in his word I hope.

Psalm 130, verses 3, 4 and 5

Following Jesus

Before you are saved, *you live for yourself* following the muddled ways of the world.
After you are saved, *you live for Jesus*, following God's good purpose for your life.

And Jesus came and said to them, "All authority in heaven and on earth has been given me. Go therefore and make disciples of all nations, baptizing them in the name of the Father and of the Son and of the Holy Spirit, teaching them to observe all that I have commanded you. And behold, I am with you always, to the end of the age."
Matthew chapter 28, verses 18 to 20

The world is all muddled and troubled because the world does not believe in the one true God.

Some people will never believe:
- Some people don't want to know the truth, because the truth is *inconvenient*: they like how they live, and don't want to change.
- Some people are *afraid* of the truth: if there is no God, then there are no rules; and if there are no rules, then there is no punishment.
- Some people simply can't *hear* the truth: it doesn't matter how you tell them, they will always remain deaf to the truth.
- Some people will be completely committed to a *false* religion, and they will argue that they are right, and you are wrong.

And since they did not see fit to acknowledge God, God gave them up to a debased mind to do what ought not to be done.
Romans chapter 1, verse 28

Living in the world, but not following the world is challenging.

For all that is in the world – the desires of the flesh and the desires of the eyes and pride in possessions – is not from the Father but is from the world.
1 John chapter 2, verse 16

You will naturally hate to hear God's truth being mocked; and you will hate to hear the name of Jesus being used as a curse word.

When everyone is ordered to follow rules that you know that God hates, you will naturally want to follow Jesus, the way that is true.

Your friends will think that you are silly because you naturally won't want to do some of the things that they all do, because those may be things that makes God unhappy.

Be renewed in the spirit of your mind, and put on the new self, created after the likeness of God in true righteousness and holiness.
Ephesians chapter 4, verses 23 and 24

Sharing the good news

God's good news is the same for everyone. But only a few will follow.

- God knows the people who will reject the truth.
- God knows the people who will follow until it becomes difficult, and then return to the world.
- God knows the people who will follow until the pleasures of the world pull them away again.
- And, God knows the people who will hear the truth, and follow Jesus, and fulfil God's good purpose for their life.

People who know you will notice a change in your nature. Do not be embarrassed to tell them why you have changed.

But in your hearts honour Christ the Lord as holy, always being prepared to make a defence to anyone who asks you for a reason for the hope that is in you; yet do with gentleness and respect.
1 Peter chapter 3, verse 15

God's purpose for you

Your life will always be filled with decisions; and if you are following Jesus you will want to make the choices that Jesus wants you to make: which career; where to live; who to marry; *etc, etc, etc,*...???

Following Jesus doesn't mean that you must become a monk, or a missionary. Following Jesus means *living in* the world, but *not belonging to* the world.

Do not conform to the pattern of this world, but be transformed by the renewing of your mind.
Then you will be able to test and approve what God's will is – his good and pleasing and perfect will. Romans chapter 12, verse 2

Be saved

The very first thing that God wills for your life is that you are *saved* from your sins by your trust in the finished work of your Lord and Saviour, Jesus Christ.

This is good, and it is pleasing in the sight of God our Saviour, who desires all people to be saved and come to the knowledge of truth.
1 Timothy chapter 2, verses 3 and 4

There are lots of people who believe in God and Jesus, heaven and hell, and already know that Jesus was killed on a cross and came back to life. But unfortunately, many of these people are not saved!

Believing in God isn't enough.
You must be saved!

You believe that God is one; you do well. Even the demons believe – and shudder.
James chapter 2, verse 19

If you have read this far, you will already know what you need to do to be saved.

Be filled with the Holy Spirit

Being the only follower of Jesus in a classroom, crowd, or team might seem a bit scary sometimes, until you realise that *you're not alone*.

With God, you will always be in the majority.

Being Spirit-filled is to live each moment of your life with the *boldness* and *confidence* of having Jesus with you *all the time*.

**And I will ask the Father, and he will give you another Helper, to be with you for ever, even the Spirit of truth, whom the world cannot receive, because it neither sees him nor knows him.
You know him, for he dwells with you and will be in you.**
John chapter 14, verses 16 and 17

To be Spirit-filled is to live your life *with* Jesus. The way to live your life with Jesus, is to study the book that is all about Jesus: *study your Bible*.

Fill yourself with the Word of God, and be filled with the Spirit of God.

Be in control of your *self*

Temptation is everywhere.
Therefore, it is important to control your desires so that your desires are honouring God.

Control the *things that you do with your body:* avoid doing anything that you would be ashamed for Jesus to see you do.

Control the *things that you look at:* avoid looking at things that you would be ashamed for Jesus to see you looking at.

Control *the way you dress:* don't dress in a way that you would be ashamed for Jesus to see you dressed.

Control *your greed:* don't be self-centred in a way that you would be ashamed for Jesus to see you.

It is not good to eat much honey, nor is it glorious to seek one's own glory. A man without self-control is like a city broken into and left without walls.
Proverbs chapter 25, verse 27 and 28

Be obedient

People love to criticise others.
And, the world especially enjoys criticising followers of Jesus.
For this reason it is important to be seen to be obedient to your parents, and to the authorities of the world.

For this is the will of God, that by doing good you should put to silence the ignorance of foolish people. 1 Peter chapter 2, verse 15

However, if the authorities of the world order you to do something that God's word tells you not to do, it's important *not to obey the world*. This is why it is necessary for you to study your Bible: so that you will know the things that God likes, and the things that God hates.

But Peter and the apostles answered, "We must obey God rather than men."
Acts chapter 5, verse 29

Be obedient to the rules of the world, but remember: *no one* has greater authority than Jesus.

Be prepared to suffer

Following Jesus can be difficult: living a good life in a wicked world means that you should expect to suffer mockery, criticism, argument, and perhaps even injury, or arrest! But, it is not because the world hates *you*: it is because the world hates *Jesus*.

No one likes to be hated or mocked. But, Jesus suffered hatred, and even death on a cross to save you from your sins: are you willing to suffer a little for Jesus?

If the world hates you, know that it has hated me before it hated you. If you were of the world, the world would love you as its own; but because you are not of the world, but I chose you out of the world, therefore the world hates you. John chapter 15, verses 18 and 19

But remember: the world needs to know God's truth, even when the world is offended by it.

What is God's purpose for you?

God's purpose for your life is revealed to you when you have fulfilled these conditions:

Be *saved* through Jesus.
Be *filled* with the Holy Spirit.
Be *in control* of your self.
Be *obedient* to authority.
Be *prepared to suffer* for Jesus.

Fulfil these conditions, and God's will for your life is: *Your desire!*

It is your desire, because it will be your new nature to desire the things that God wants for your life.

**Delight yourself in the Lord; trust in him, and he will give you the desires of your heart.
Commit your way to the Lord; trust in him, and he will act.**
Psalm 37, verses 4 and 5

When you follow Jesus, whatever you desire is God's will for your life, because you will be led by God's word and the Holy Spirit to make the correct decisions for your life.

Make me to know your ways, O Lord; teach me your paths.
Lead me in your truth and teach me, for you are the God of my salvation; for you I wait all the day long. Psalm 25, verses 4 and 5

You might desire to be: a doctor, or a gardener; an airplane pilot, or a bus driver; a mechanic, or a missionary; a business owner; or to stay at home to raise your children.
(It was my desire to leave my busy job in Belfast to write this book that you are reading now, because it is my great desire for you to be saved.)

Whatever you decide to do, and in whichever direction God's Spirit might *redirect* you, know that God will use you wherever you are.

Whatever you do, work heartily, as for the Lord and not for men, knowing that from the Lord you will receive the inheritance as your reward.
You are serving the Lord Christ.
Colossians chapter 3, verses 23 and 24

Any questions

I love to learn from my Bible.
And, I have also learnt that there is no such thing as a silly question if it prevents you from making a silly mistake.

If you have any questions about *anything* in the Bible, please search for answers.

Ask a church leader to help you; and, if you are not sure about his answer, ask another leader.
(Just tell them that I sent you.)

And, make sure that they explain the answers *from the Bible* in a way that you can clearly understand.

The beginning of wisdom is this: get wisdom, and whatever you get, get insight.

Proverbs chapter 4, verse 7

Be blessed

May God bless you as you *submit yourself* to follow Jesus.

May your walk with God be blessed with ever-growing confidence in the *truth* that Jesus has defeated sin and death for everyone who believes.

May God bless you with a happy spirit so that you may *shine* God's loving light into this dark world.

May God bless you with his loving-kindness and tender mercies, so that you *never need to worry* about how you will deal with tomorrow.

May God bless you with *confidence* in his Holy Spirit: that God may *speak* through you, and *work* through you, so that you will fulfil God's good purpose for your life.

The grace of the Lord Jesus Christ and the love of God and the fellowship of the Holy Spirit be with you

2 Corinthians chapter 13, verse 14

Suggested reading

On page 69 I suggested that you read one book of the Bible once a day for 30 days in a row, which will help you to establish God's word in your heart and mind.

I recommended that you read 1 John, which is the first letter that John wrote to the gatherings of new believers in Jesus.
His letter contains many important gospel truths that have been covered in this book.

John was chosen by Jesus, and remained with him throughout the three years when Jesus was teaching and working miracles. John knew Jesus personally, and followed Jesus closely as his beloved teacher.
John also wrote two very important books in the Bible: the gospel according to **John**, and the **Revelation**.

John's letter is just five short chapters, and you can read it end-to-end in about 30-minutes.

1 John

Throughout this book I have chosen to use the *English Standard Version* of the Bible because the translation holds its integrity from the original Hebrew, Greek, and Aramaic scriptures, and the language is more accessible for young people to understand than older traditional translations.

In the following scripture I have added words and phrases ([*in bracketed italics*]) to help with clarity.

In accordance with the conditions of the publisher of the *English Standard Version* of the Bible, 1 John has not been reproduced in its entirety: verses 16 and 17 of chapter 5 have been omitted, and you can read these for yourself in your own Bible.

1 John

From the *English Standard Version* of the Bible
[*words in bracketed italics have been added*]

1.

That [*that is, the Son of God*] which was from the beginning, which we have heard, which we have seen with our [*own*] eyes, which we looked upon and have touched with our [*own*] hands, concerning the word of life— the life was made manifest (*revealed to us*), and we have seen it [*as eye-witnesses*], and testify to it (*swear to it*) and proclaim to you the eternal life [*Jesus Christ*], which was [*already existing*] with the Father and was made manifest to us [*in human form*]— that which we have seen and heard we proclaim also to you, so that you too may have fellowship [*as fellow believers*] with us; and indeed our fellowship is with the Father and with his Son Jesus Christ.

And we are writing these things so that our joy may be complete [*by sharing this truth with you*].

This is the message we have heard from him and proclaim to you, that God is light [*pure, holy and true*], and in him is no darkness [*no sin, no wickedness nor imperfection*] at all.

If we say we have fellowship with him while we walk in darkness [*following the ways of the world*], we lie and do not practice the truth. But if we walk in the light [*truly following the way of Jesus*], as he is in the light, we have fellowship with one another, and the blood [*poured out during his death on a cross*] of Jesus his Son cleanses us from all sin [*paying in full the punishment that we deserve for our sins*].

If we say we have no sin, we deceive ourselves, and the truth is not in us. If we confess our sins, he is faithful and just to forgive us our sins and to cleanse us from all unrighteousness (*from our sinful nature*). If we say we have not sinned (*if we refuse to confess that we are sinners*), we make him a liar, and his word is not in us.

2.

My little children (*new believers*), I am writing these things to you so that you may not sin. But if anyone does sin, we have an advocate [*the person who will speak on our behalf*] with the Father, Jesus Christ the righteous [*the Son of God who is without sin, and obedient to his Father's will and purpose*]. He is the propitiation (*the means by which the anger of God is turned away from us*) for our sins, and not for ours only but also for the sins of the whole world (*the sins of everyone who puts their trust in the finished work of Jesus*).

And by this we know that we have come to know him, if we keep his commandments (*if we follow the teachings of Jesus*).

Whoever says "I know him" but does not keep his commandments is a liar, and the truth is not in him, but whoever keeps his word [*in obedience to the teachings of Jesus*], in him truly the love of God is perfected.

By this we may know that we are in him: whoever says he abides (*lives in obedient fellowship*) in him (*Jesus*) ought to walk (*live*) in the same way in which he (*Jesus*) walked.

Beloved (*dearest brothers- and sisters-in-Christ*), I am writing you no new commandment, but an old commandment that you had from the beginning. The old commandment is the word that you have heard. At the same time, it is a new commandment that I am writing to you, which is true in him and in you, because the darkness [*of the sinful world*] is passing away and the true light [*of God's truth*] is already shining.

Whoever says he is in the light and hates his brother (*fellow believer in Jesus Christ*) is still in darkness (*following the sinful world*). Whoever loves his brother abides in the light, and in him there is no cause for stumbling. But whoever hates his brother is in the darkness [*of the sinful world*] and walks in the darkness [*following the sinful ways of the world*], and does not know where he is going, because the darkness [*of the sinful world*] has blinded his eyes.

I am writing to you, little children, because your sins are forgiven for his name's sake (*because you have confessed Jesus Christ as your Lord and Saviour*).

I am writing to you, fathers, because you know him who is from the beginning.

I am writing to you, young men, because you have overcome the evil one.

I write to you, children, because you know the Father.

I write to you, fathers, because you know him who is from the beginning.

I write to you, young men, because you are strong, and the word of God abides in you, and [*through your union with Jesus Christ*] you have overcome the evil one.

Do not love the world or the things in the world [*that reject Jesus and oppose God*]. If anyone loves the world, the love of the Father is not in him. For all that is in the world— the desires of the flesh (*physical pleasures*) and the desires of the eyes (*worldly possessions*) and pride of life (*boasting of personal achievements*)—is not from the Father but is from the world. And the world is passing away (*coming to an end*) along with its desires, but whoever does the will of God abides (*lives with God*) forever.

Children, it is the last hour (*the time immediately before the return of Jesus Christ, and the Judgement of sinners*), and as you have heard that antichrist (*a person who denies that Jesus is the Son of God*) is coming, so now many antichrists have come. Therefore we know that it is the last hour. They (*these people who reject Jesus Christ as the Son of God*) went out from us [teaching lies about who Jesus truly is], but they were not of us; for if they had been of us, they would have continued (*remained*) with us. But they went out, that it might become plain that they all are not of us.

But you have been anointed [chosen, and set apart] by the Holy One, and you all have knowledge [of the truth that Jesus truly is the Son of God].

I write to you, not because you do not know the truth, but because you know it, and because no lie is of the truth. Who is the liar but he who denies that Jesus is the Christ [*the chosen One, the only Son of God*]? This is the antichrist, he who denies the Father and the Son. No one who denies the Son has the Father. Whoever confesses the Son has the Father also.

Let what you heard from the beginning abide (*remain*) in you. If what you heard from the beginning abides in you, then you too will abide in the Son and in the Father. And this is the promise that he made to us—eternal life.

I write these things to you about those who are trying to deceive you [*to lead you away from the truth*]. But the anointing [*gift of the Holy Spirit*] that you received from him abides in you, and you have no need that anyone should teach you. But as his anointing teaches you [*through the insight given to you by the Holy Spirit*] about everything, and is true, and is no lie—just as it has taught you, abide in him.

And now, little children, abide in him [*with unwavering faith*], so that when he appears we may have confidence and not shrink from him in shame at his coming. If you know that he is righteous, you may be sure that everyone who practices righteousness [*following the teachings of Jesus, and conforming to God's will*] has been born of him (*has been reborn through Jesus Christ*).

3.

See what kind of love the Father has given to us, that we should be called children of God; and so we are. The reason why the world does not know us is that it did not know him (*Jesus*). Beloved, we are God's children now, and what we will be [*when Jesus Christ returns*] has not yet appeared; but we know that when he appears (*returns*) we shall be like him, because we shall see him as he is [*in all of His heavenly glory*]. And everyone who thus hopes in him (*who share the eager expectation of the return of Jesus*) purifies himself as he (*Jesus*) is pure.

Everyone who makes a practice of sinning also practices lawlessness (*ignoring God's law, tolerating sin, not following Jesus*); sin is lawlessness. You know that he [*the Son of God*] appeared [*as the man Jesus, who suffered and died on a cross*] in order to take away sins, and in him there is no sin. No one who abides in him keeps on sinning; no one who keeps on sinning has either seen him or known (*understood*) him. Little children, let no one deceive you. Whoever practices righteousness is righteous, as he (*Jesus*) is righteous. Whoever makes a practice of sinning is of the devil, for the devil has been sinning from the beginning. The reason the Son of God appeared was to destroy the works of the devil (*to remove sin and the curse of death*). No one born of God makes a practice of sinning, for God's seed abides in him, and he cannot keep on sinning because he has been born (*born again*) of God. By this it is evident who are the children of God, and who are the children of the devil: whoever does not practice righteousness is not of God, nor is the one who does not love his brother (*fellow believer in Jesus Christ*).

For this is the message that you have heard from the beginning, that we should love one another. We should not be like Cain (*see: Genesis chapter 4, verses 8 to 10*), who was of the evil one and murdered his brother [*Abel*]. And why did he murder him? Because his own deeds were evil and his brother's righteous.
Do not be surprised, brothers (*fellow believers*), that the world hates you. We know that we have passed out of death into life, because we love the brothers (*each other*). Whoever does not love abides in death. Everyone who hates his brother is a murderer [*in his heart*], and you know that no murderer has eternal life abiding in him.

By this we know love, that he (*the Son of God*) laid down his life (*left his throne in heaven to come to earth to sacrifice his own life*) for us, and we ought to lay down our lives for the brothers (*fellow believers*). But if anyone has the world's goods (*enough money or possessions*) and sees his brother in need, yet closes his heart against him (*shows no pity, and refuses to help*), how does God's love abide in him?
Little children, let us not love in word or talk, but in deed and in truth. By this we shall know that we are of the truth and reassure our heart

before him; for whenever our heart condemns us (*whenever we remember our failures and realise that we are guilty of sin*), God is greater than our heart, and he knows everything (*no secret thing about us is hidden from God*).

Beloved, if our heart does not condemn us, we have confidence (*through Jesus, who paid in full the punishment for our sins*) before God; and whatever we ask we receive from him, because we keep his commandments and do what pleases him.

And this is his (*God's*) commandment, that we believe in the name of his Son Jesus Christ and love one another, just as he has commanded us. Whoever keeps (*obeys*) his commandments abides in God, and God in him. And by this we know that he abides in us, by the Spirit (*the Holy Spirit that dwells within believers*) whom he has given us.

4.

Beloved, do not believe every spirit [*that speaks through a self-proclaimed prophet*], but test the spirits [*against the truth of the Bible*] to see whether they are from God, for many false prophets (*untruthful teachers who spread lies and deceive people*) have gone out into the world.

By this you know the Spirit of God: every spirit that confesses that Jesus Christ has come in the flesh is from God, and every spirit that does not confess Jesus is not from God. This is the spirit of the antichrist (*the person who rejects the truth that Jesus is the Son of God*), which you heard was coming and now is in the world already [*spreading lies about Jesus*].

Little children (*new believers*), you are from God and have overcome them (*the people who lie about Jesus*), for he who is in you (*the Holy Spirit*) is greater than he [*the devil*] who is in the world [*of sin*]. They are from the world; therefore they speak from the world, and the world listens to them (*people will believe what they want to believe, and behave how they want to behave*). We are from God. Whoever knows God listens to us; whoever is not from God does not listen to us. By this we know the Spirit of truth and the spirit of error [*deception and lies*].

Beloved (*fellow believers*), let us love one another (*care about each other, and care for each other with genuine compassion and selfless generosity*), for love is from God, and whoever loves has been born of God and knows God. Anyone who does not love does not know God, because God is love. In this the love of God was made manifest among us (*in the person of Jesus Christ*), that God sent his only Son into the world, so that we might live [*eternally*] through him.

In this is love, not that we have loved God but that he loved us and sent his Son to be the propitiation [*the perfect sin-cleansing blood sacrifice*] for our sins. Beloved, if God so loved us, we also ought to love one another.

No one has ever seen God; if we love one another, God abides in us and his love is perfected in us. By this [*love for each other*] we know that we abide in him and he in us, because he has given us of his Spirit [*who dwells within us*]. And we have seen and testify that the Father has sent his Son to be the Saviour of the world. Whoever confesses that Jesus is the Son of God, God abides in him, and he in God. So we have come to know and to believe the love that God has for us.

God is love, and whoever abides in love abides in God, and God abides in him [*in the person of the Holy Spirit*]. By this is love perfected with us, so that we may have confidence for the day of judgment [*when all people will stand before God to be judged for their sins*], because as he is [*sinless*] so also are we in this world (*because of the death, burial and resurrection of Jesus, we are made as perfect and sinless as Jesus*). There is no fear in love, but perfect love casts out fear. For fear has to do with punishment [*of the Judgement of sinners*], and whoever fears [*the Judgement of sinners*] has not been perfected in love (*has not properly understood God's love toward them*). We love because he first loved us (*God loved you before you were conceived in your mother's womb; before you were saved, even then, God loved you).*

If anyone says, "I love God," and hates his brother *(fellow believer)*, he is a liar; for he who does not love his brother whom he has seen cannot love God whom he has not seen. And this commandment we have from him: whoever loves God must also love his brother *(fellow believer in Jesus Christ)*.

5.

Everyone who believes that Jesus is the Christ has been born of God, and everyone who loves the Father loves whoever has been born of him. By this we know that we love the children of God, when we love God and obey his commandments. For this is the love of God, that we keep his commandments. And his commandments are not burdensome *(they are not difficult to obey)*. For everyone who has been born of God overcomes the world *(Jesus has conquered sin and death, which means that there is nothing that you need to fear from the world)*. And this is the victory that has overcome the world—our faith *(our belief and trust in the finished work of Jesus)*.

Who is it that overcomes the world except the one who believes that Jesus is the Son of God?

This is he (*the Son of God*) who came by water (*representing the immortal spiritual nature of Jesus*) and blood (*representing the mortal human person of Jesus*)—Jesus Christ; not by the water only but by the water and the blood (*when Jesus was killed on a cross, a soldier pierced Jesus' side with a spear to make sure that he was definitely dead: blood and water flowed from Jesus' side*). And the Spirit is the one who testifies, because the Spirit is the truth. For there are three that testify: the Spirit and the water and the blood; and these three agree (*Jesus was proven to be killed beyond doubt, but came back to life three days later, defeating the curse of death – this is what we believe*). If we receive the testimony (*word*) of men, the testimony (*word*) of God is greater, for this is the testimony of God that he has borne concerning his Son.

Whoever believes in the Son of God has the testimony in himself (*can speak with confidence about the change that Jesus Christ has made in his life*). Whoever does not believe God has made him (*God*) a liar, because he has not believed in the testimony that God has borne concerning his Son. And this is the testimony, that God gave us eternal life, and this life is in his Son. Whoever has the Son has life; whoever does not have the Son of God does not have life (*Jesus is the only person who can save you from your sins, and from death*).

I write these things to you who believe in the name of the Son of God that you may know that you have eternal life. And this is the confidence that we have toward him, that if we ask anything according to his will (*agreeable to God's purpose*) he hears us. And if we know that he hears us in whatever we ask, we know that we have the requests that we have asked of him.

We know that everyone who has been born of God does not keep on sinning, but he who was born of God protects him, and the evil one does not touch him. We know that we are from God, and the whole world lies in the power [*misery and influence*] of the evil one. And we know that the Son of God has come and has given us understanding, so that we may know him (*Jesus Christ*) who is true; and we are in him who is true, in his Son Jesus Christ. He is the true God and eternal life.

Little children, keep yourselves from idols (*keep yourselves from worshipping anything except the one true God*).

The Lord bless you
and keep you;

The Lord make his face
to shine upon you
and be gracious to you;

The Lord lift up his
countenance upon you
and give you peace.

Numbers chapter 6, verses 24 to 26

Printed by Amazon Italia Logistica S.r.l.
Torrazza Piemonte (TO), Italy